Emma Stone

ABDO
Publishing Company

Big Buddy BOOKS
Buddy Bios

by Sarah Tieck

VISIT US AT
www.abdopublishing.com

Published by ABDO Publishing Company, PO Box 398166, Minneapolis, Minnesota 55439.

Copyright © 2014 by Abdo Consulting Group, Inc. International copyrights reserved in all countries. No part of this book may be reproduced in any form without written permission from the publisher. Big Buddy Books™ is a trademark and logo of ABDO Publishing Company.

Printed in the United States of America, North Mankato, Minnesota.
052013
092013

PRINTED ON RECYCLED PAPER

Coordinating Series Editor: Rochelle Baltzer
Contributing Editors: Megan M. Gunderson, Marcia Zappa
Graphic Design: Maria Hosley
Cover Photograph: *AP Photo*: Rex Features via AP Images.
Interior Photographs/Illustrations: *AP Photo*: Evan Agostini (p. 9), AP Photo (p. 9), Anthony Behar/Sipa USA (Sipa via AP Images) (p. 27), Luis Martinez (p. 13), Chris Pizzello (p. 17), Sony Pictures/Jack Plunkett (p. 15), Rex Features via AP Images (pp. 18, 21, 25), Matt Sayles (pp. 11, 15), Markus Schreiber (p. 5); *Getty Images*: Neilson Barnard/Getty Images (p. 29), Jon Kopaloff/FilmMagic (p. 9), Jeff Kravitz/FilmMagic (p. 23), Ethan Miller (p. 7).

Library of Congress Control Number: 2012956014

Cataloging-in-Publication Data

Tieck, Sarah.
 Emma Stone: talented actress / Sarah Tieck.
   p. cm. -- (Big buddy biographies)
 ISBN 978-1-61783-861-3
 1. Stone, Emma, 1988- --Juvenile literature. 2. Actors--United States--Biography--Juvenile literature. 3. Singers--United States--Biography--Juvenile literature. I. Title.
 791.4302--dc23
 [B]   2012956014

Emma Stone

Contents

Screen Star 4
Family Ties 6
Improv Acting 8
Early Years 10
Making Movies 14
New Direction 19
Big Opportunities 20
An Actress's Life 22
Off the Screen 26
Buzz 28
Snapshot 30
Important Words 31
Web Sites 31
Index 32

> Emma is known for being funny. But she has had more serious parts, too.

Screen Star

Emma Stone is a talented actress. She has appeared in several movies and television shows. She is known as one of the stars of *The Amazing Spider-Man*. And, she was the voice of a character in *The Croods*.

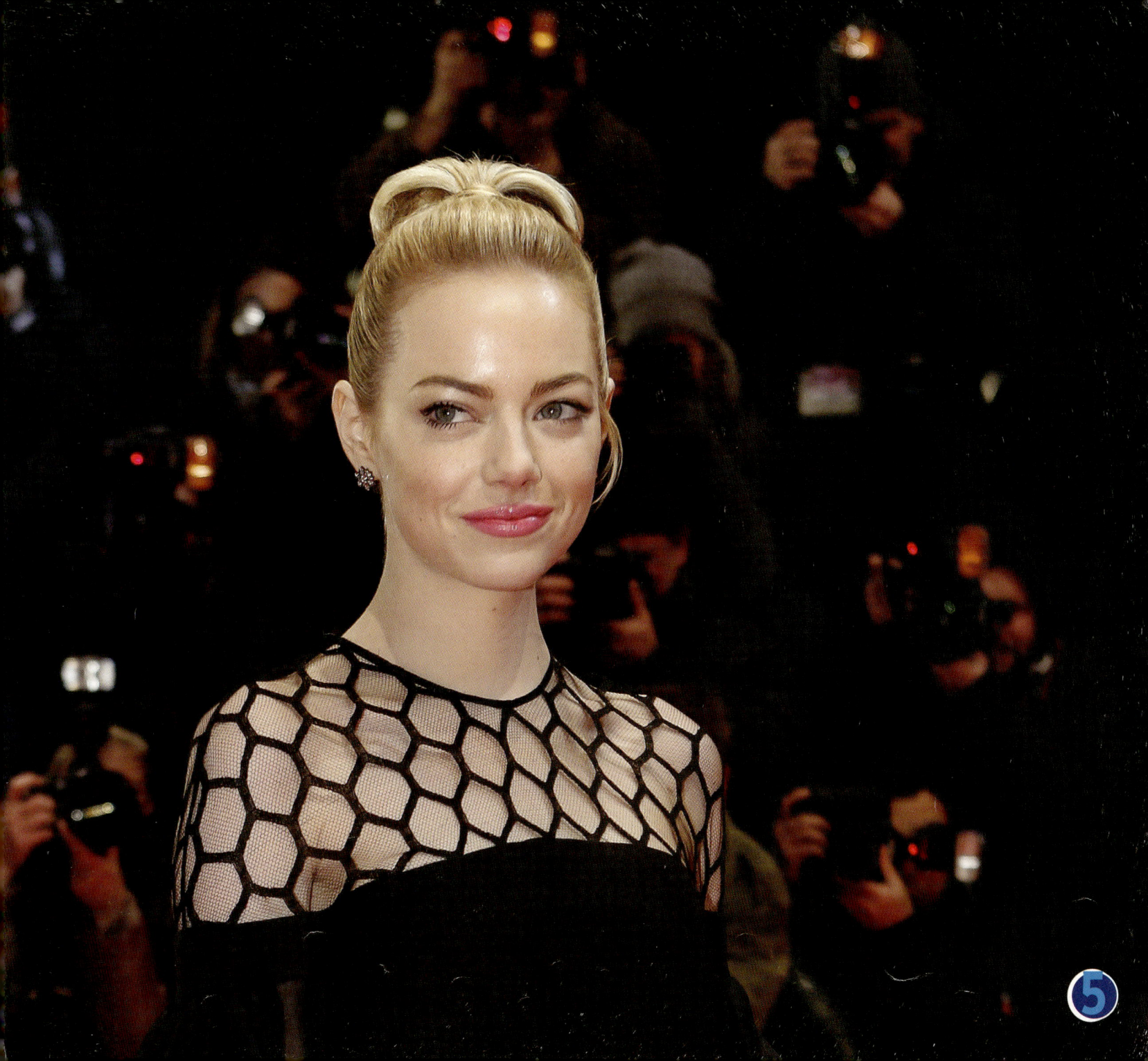

Where in the World?

Did you know...
Emma and her dad enjoyed watching *The Jerk* starring Steve Martin.

Family Ties

Emily Jean "Emma" Stone was born in Scottsdale, Arizona, on November 6, 1988. Emma's parents are Krista and Jeff Stone. Emma's brother is Spencer. Emma's parents owned a golf course. Her dad enjoyed funny movies. He taught her to love them, too.

Sometimes Spencer or other family members attend events with Emma.

Improv Acting

Emma learned acting skills by doing improvisational, or improv, acting. In this type of theater, people act without a **script**.

Improv shows are often funny. Actors work together to build skills that help them act in the moment. Sometimes, they do live **performances**.

Emma often did improv acting at Valley Youth Theatre in Phoenix.

Emma admires the work of actors such as John Candy (*left*) and Steve Martin (*above*). Both are known for comedy and improv acting.

Early Years

> **Did you know...**
> Emma made a PowerPoint presentation to convince her parents to move to California. Emma felt she could grow as an actress there.

Emma had wanted to be an actress since she was young. So, she worked on it in small ways. She acted in many theater shows.

Around 2000, Emma asked her parents to be homeschooled. That way, she could attend **auditions**.

Emma and her mom moved to Los Angeles, California, around 2003. There, she tried out for television parts, including many Disney shows. She was disappointed because she didn't get any parts.

Emma's mom has always supported her daughter's work.

Soon, Emma began to get **roles**. In 2004 and 2005, she worked on several small parts. She met people who helped her get more work.

In 2006, Emma had small parts on *The Suite Life of Zack and Cody* and *Malcolm in the Middle*. In 2007, she got her first regular role on a show called *Drive*. She continued to try out for many parts, including movie roles.

Emma often changes her hair color for her roles. It has been brown, blonde, and red!

13

Making Movies

Emma worked with Jesse Eisenberg (*left*) and Woody Harrelson (*right*) in *Zombieland*.

In 2007, Emma appeared in her first movie. It was a **comedy** called *Superbad*. People noticed that Emma was a talented, funny actress.

Because the movie did well, Emma began to have more opportunities. In 2008 and 2009, she appeared in *The Rocker* and *Zombieland*. In 2010, she provided a voice in *Marmaduke*. Each movie helped her grow as an actress.

Superbad was a movie about friendship. Emma had a supporting part in the movie.

Emma was up for a Golden Globe Award for her acting in *Easy A*. Even though she didn't win, she was honored to be included.

In 2010, Emma got her first starring **role**! It was in a movie called *Easy A*. Emma stood out as a talented actress. There were even news stories about her great acting.

That same year, Emma was asked to host *Saturday Night Live*. She was very excited! She said it was like a dream coming true.

In *The Help*, Skeeter is a writer. She wants to tell the stories of people who are being treated unfairly.

Did you know...
The Help is set in the 1960s. It takes place during the civil rights movement.

New Direction

In 2011, Emma appeared in two hit movies. These were *Crazy, Stupid, Love* and *The Help*.

In *The Help*, Emma plays a character named Skeeter Phelan. This was an important **role** for her. It was the first time she'd starred in a **drama** or in such a big movie.

> **Did you know...**
> In *The Amazing Spider-Man*, Emma's hair was blonde. This is her real hair color!

Big Opportunities

In 2012, Emma acted in *The Amazing Spider-Man*. This movie is about Peter Parker becoming Spider-Man.

Emma plays Gwen Stacy, who falls in love with Peter Parker. Emma got ready for her part by reading comic books and studying her character.

Emma and her costar Andrew Garfield became close friends. Andrew plays Peter Parker.

Did you know...

Emma knows sign language. She uses it to improve her acting. She says it helps her use body language, which is important for acting.

An Actress's Life

As an actress, Emma spends time practicing **lines** and **performing**. She may be on a movie **set** for several hours each day.

Some of this time is spent filming. And, some of it is spent getting ready. Actresses and actors put on special makeup and clothing to look more like their characters.

In 2012, Emma and Andrew presented a Nickelodeon Kids' Choice Award.

Emma signs autographs and takes pictures with fans.

Emma also attends events and meets fans. Sometimes, she travels to make or **promote** her movies. She may be away from home for several days or even months.

In June 2012, Emma and Andrew helped a Boys and Girls Club in New York. The event raised money to fight cancer.

Off the Screen

When Emma is not working, she enjoys being at home. She spends time with her family, friends, and dogs. She is also interested in reading and fashion.

Emma likes to help others. Her parents taught her about **volunteering**. She attends events that raise money for certain causes. These include **cancer**, education, and homelessness.

Buzz

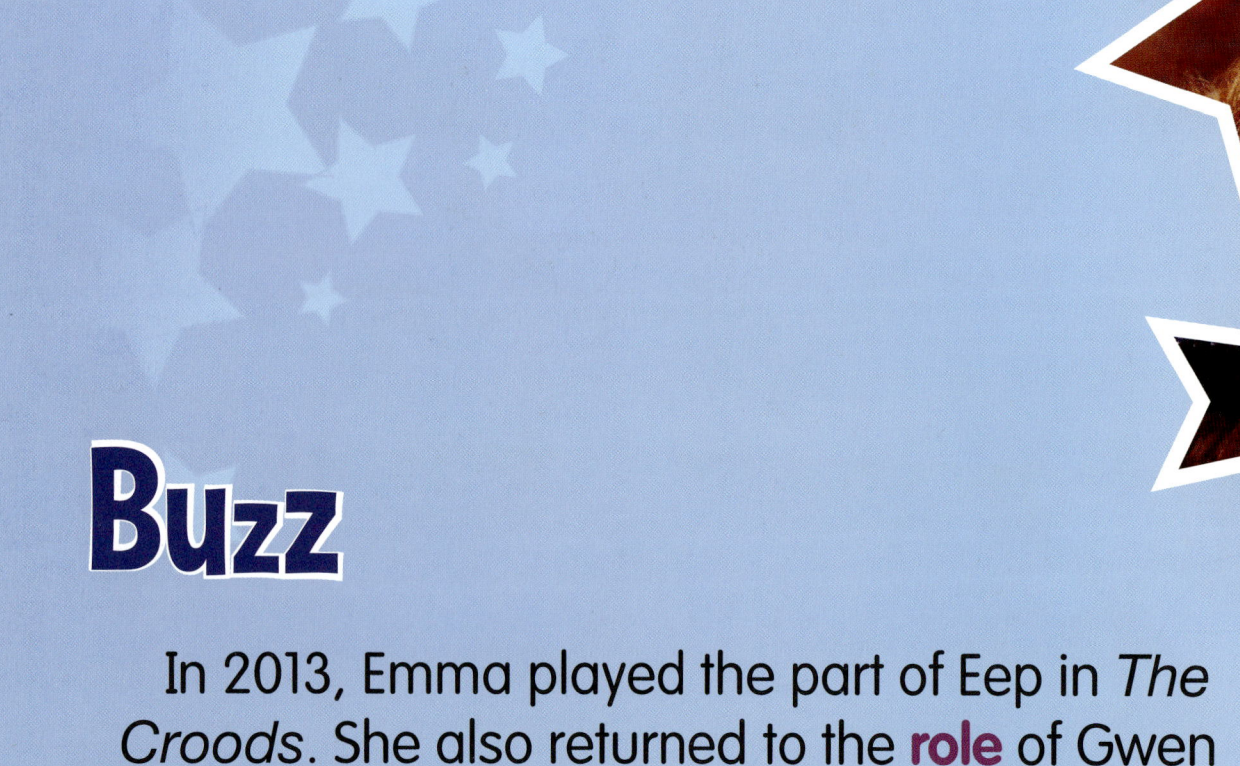

In 2013, Emma played the part of Eep in *The Croods*. She also returned to the **role** of Gwen Stacy to film *The Amazing Spider-Man 2*.

Emma's fame continues to grow. Fans look forward to what's next for her! Many believe she has a bright **future**.

Emma used different skills to do voice acting in *The Croods*.

Snapshot

★ **Name**: Emily Jean "Emma" Stone

★ **Birthday**: November 6, 1988

★ **Birthplace**: Scottsdale, Arizona

★ **Appearances**: The Suite Life of Zack and Cody, Malcolm in the Middle, Drive, Superbad, The Rocker, Zombieland, Marmaduke, Easy A, Saturday Night Live, Crazy, Stupid, Love, The Help, The Amazing Spider-Man, The Croods, The Amazing Spider-Man 2

Important Words

audition (aw-DIH-shuhn) a trial performance showcasing personal talent as a musician, a singer, a dancer, or an actor.
cancer any of a group of very harmful diseases that cause a body's cells to become unhealthy.
comedy a funny story.
drama a play, movie, or television show that is about something serious.
future (FYOO-chuhr) a time that has not yet occurred.
lines the words an actor says in a play, a movie, or a show.
perform to do something in front of an audience. A performance is the act of doing something, such as singing or acting, in front of an audience.
promote to help something become known.
role a part an actor plays.
script the written text of a play, movie, or television show.
set the place where a movie or a television show is recorded.
volunteer (vah-luhn-TIHR) to help others in one's free time without pay.

Web Sites

To learn more about Emma Stone, visit ABDO Publishing Company online. Web sites about Emma Stone are featured on our Book Links page. These links are routinely monitored and updated to provide the most current information available.

www.abdopublishing.com

Index

Amazing Spider-Man, The (movie) **4, 20, 30**

Amazing Spider-Man 2, The (movie) **28, 30**

Arizona **6, 9, 30**

California **10**

Candy, John **9**

charity work **26**

Crazy, Stupid, Love (movie) **19, 30**

Croods, The (movie) **4, 28, 29, 30**

Drive (television show) **12, 30**

Easy A (movie) **16, 30**

education **10**

Eisenberg, Jesse **14**

Garfield, Andrew **21, 23, 26**

Harrelson, Woody **14**

Help, The (movie) **18, 19, 30**

Jerk, The (movie) **6**

Malcolm in the Middle (television show) **12, 30**

Marmaduke (movie) **14, 30**

Martin, Steve **6, 9**

New York **26**

Rocker, The (movie) **14, 30**

Saturday Night Live (television show) **16, 30**

Stone, Jeff **6, 7, 10, 26**

Stone, Krista **6, 7, 10, 11, 26**

Stone, Spencer **6, 7, 26**

Suite Life of Zack and Cody, The (television show) **12, 30**

Superbad (movie) **14, 15, 30**

Zombieland (movie) **14, 30**

Robert B. Turner Elementary
1411 Fox Creek Road
Lawrenceburg, KY 40342